## DATE DUE

# Roald
# Dahl

# Roald
# Dahl

## Adam Woog

**KIDHAVEN PRESS**

*An imprint of Thomson Gale, a part of The Thomson Corporation*

**THOMSON**
✦
**GALE**

Detroit • New York • San Francisco • San Diego • New Haven, Conn. • Waterville, Maine • London • Munich

This is for Leah, who is the biggest Roald Dahl fan in
our family now that she has gotten so tall.

© 2005 Thomson Gale, a part of The Thomson Corporation.

Thomson, Star Logo and KidHaven Press are trademarks and Gale is a registered trademark
used herein under license.

*For more information, contact*
KidHaven Press
27500 Drake Rd.
Farmington Hills, MI 48331-3535
Or you can visit our Internet site at http://www.gale.com

LIBRARY OF CONGRESS CATALOGING-IN-PUBLICATION DATA

Woog, Adam, 1953–
    Roald Dahl / by Adam Woog.
        p. cm. — (Inventors and creators)
    ISBN 0-7377-2614-8
Summary: Discusses children's book author Roald Dahl including his childhood, his
time spent in the military, his marriages and children, his books and screenplays,
and the film and stage versions of his books.
    1. Dahl, Roald—Childhood and youth—Juvenile literature.  2. Authors, English—
20th century—Biography—Juvenile literature.  3. Children's stories—Authorship—
Juvenile literature.  I. Title.  II. Series.
    PR6054.A35Z95 2005
    823'.914—dc22

                                                                            2004002667

Printed in the United States of America

# Contents

# The Champion Storyteller

Roald Dahl was one of the most creative and popular writers of children's books who ever lived. He had millions of fans around the world when he was alive. He has even more today.

When his fans discover Dahl, they eagerly read his most famous works, such as *Charlie and the Chocolate Factory* and *James and the Giant Peach*. They devour his many other books, including *Matilda, The BFG,* and *The Witches.* Then they want more.

## "I Know What Children Like"

Kids love Roald Dahl's books for many reasons. First of all, he used strong, colorful language to tell thrilling stories. Something wonderful is always happening in a Dahl book. As the author once remarked, "I only write about things that are exciting or funny."[1]

Another reason that Dahl's books are appealing is because his characters show strong emotions. Some characters are naughty, selfish, thoughtless, or cruel.

Others are warm, funny, inventive, or wise. Often his most interesting characters are both a little good and a little bad—just like people in real life.

Dahl also knew what captures the attention of young readers. For example, he understood that kids love to read about other kids in danger. So the young heroes in his books usually have to overcome fearsome foes. For

Roald Dahl was one of the world's most imaginative writers of children's books.

instance, in *The Witches* a seven-year-old boy battles a convention of creepy witches who are out to get him.

Furthermore, Dahl loved telling stories in which children battle ugly, mean grown-ups. In books such as *Matilda,* kids find clever ways to get even with these horrible adults. Dahl always said that the key to his suc-

The Grand High Witch from the 1990 film version of *The Witches* looks very wicked.

cess was that he was on the side of the kids in his books. "Parents and schoolteachers," he said of the adult characters, "are the enemy."[2]

Many adults enjoy Dahl's books as much as kids do. However, some parents dislike them. These adults think his books are too violent and that his wicked characters are bad influences on young people.

Such criticisms never bothered Dahl. In his opinion, kids understand that life is not always totally fair or completely happy. He once remarked, "I never get any protests from children. . . . I know what children like."[3]

## Being "Sparky"

Dahl worked hard to fill his books with excitement and wonder. One of the most important things, he often said, was to be "sparky." He meant that it is important to be curious and to make others curious about the world around them.

In his personal life Dahl was just as eager to create excitement. He was always finding some adventure to share with his family, especially his children. Perhaps it was exploring a country meadow, feeding a farm animal, or simply flying a kite. Whatever the activity, Dahl worked hard to make it interesting. The writer's second wife, Felicity Dahl, recalls, "There was never a moment when he wasn't inventing or making life fun."[4]

But Dahl was not a perfect person. Sometimes he could be as unkind as one of the awful adults in his stories. He knew a lot about many things, and he liked to show off that knowledge. He always felt the need to

Dahl and his family enjoy an afternoon in the English countryside in this 1961 photo.

be in control, which also upset some people. He was even mischievous, and his eagerness to stir things up sometimes caused trouble.

Despite his faults, Dahl was never boring. The story of his life had many high points and quite a bit of sadness. That life began in a small town in Wales.

# Chapter One

# A Boy in Wales

R oald grew up in Wales, which is part of Great Britain. His parents were from Norway. His father, Harald, had left Norway as a young man. He worked as a ship's broker, someone who provides ships with supplies.

Harald settled in the 1880s in Cardiff, the largest city in Wales. Cardiff was a port and an important center for coal, which steamships needed for fuel. It was a good place for a ship's broker.

## Norwegians in Wales

As a boy Harald Dahl had broken one of his arms. The doctor who tried to fix it was clumsy, and he set the arm improperly. Because of the doctor's failure, Harald's arm had to be cut off. With only one arm, Harald could still do most things well. He loved to garden and he collected rare plants. He was an expert wood carver. He said that the only thing he could not do by himself was cut the top off a soft-boiled egg.

Harald's business did well, and he bought a large house in Llandaff, a village near Cardiff. He and his

French-born wife, Marie, had two children, Louis and Ellen. Tragically, however, Marie died while giving birth to Ellen. In 1911 Harald remarried. His new wife was a Norwegian woman named Sofie Magdalene Hesselberg.

## Birth and Death

Harald and Sofie had four more children: Astri, Alfhild, Roald, and Else. Roald Dahl was born on September 13, 1916. He and his half brother, Louis, were the only boys in the family.

When Roald was two, the Dahl family moved to the nearby village of Radyr. There were now eight in the family, and Harald bought a big house with acres of land. There, Roald grew to become a tall, bright boy who loved new experiences and adventures. He was very close to everyone in his family.

Roald's first years were generally happy. However, when Roald was four, his sister Astri died of **appendicitis.** Roald's father loved Astri very much, and he was brokenhearted when she died. Harald's health declined, and within months he died of **pneumonia.**

## Beginning School

With her husband dead, Sofie Dahl became the only adult responsible for five children. She was also pregnant with another girl, Asta. She was in a strange country with no relatives nearby. Roald later wrote, "A less courageous woman would almost certainly have sold the house and packed her bags and headed straight back to Norway with the children."[5]

Roald walks with his mother Sofie near the family's home in the Welsh town of Radyr.

However, Sofie was strong. She chose to stay and fulfill Harald's wishes. He had wanted his children to attend English schools, which he thought were the best. Sofie moved the family back to Llandaff. There Roald attended Elmtree House elementary school and Llandaff Cathedral School.

Roald was only at the Cathedral School for two years, though. This was because he and some other boys played a trick on the mean owner of a candy shop. They

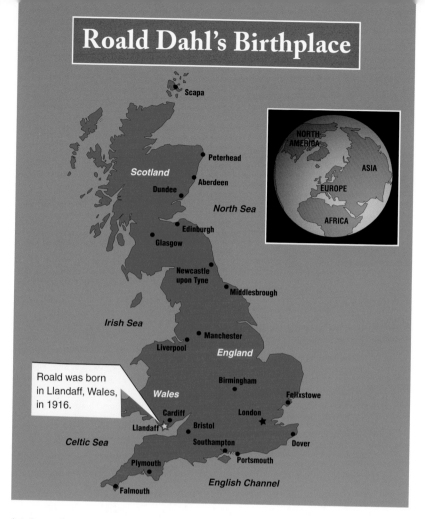

## Roald Dahl's Birthplace

Scapa

Peterhead

Scotland

Aberdeen

Dundee

North Sea

Edinburgh

Glasgow

Newcastle upon Tyne

Middlesbrough

Irish Sea

Manchester

Liverpool

England

Roald was born in Llandaff, Wales, in 1916.

Wales

Birmingham

Cardiff

Felixstowe

London

Llandaff

Bristol

Celtic Sea

Southampton

Dover

Plymouth

Portsmouth

English Channel

Falmouth

NORTH AMERICA

ASIA

EUROPE

AFRICA

hid a dead mouse in a candy jar and watched as she reached in to find it. The boys were caught and punished by being caned (beaten on the bottom with a cane). Sofie was so angry about this cruel punishment that she put Roald in a different school, St. Peter's.

## St. Peter's

St. Peter's was in a nearby town. Because of the distance from his house, Roald had to live at school. He was miserable there. He disliked being away from his family. He hated the awful meals and cruel older boys. He despised the beatings given out by teachers and **headmasters**.

Because he was so unhappy, Roald could not focus on studying. His grades were not good. He even did poorly in English class. Many years later he wrote, "Spelling was never my strong point and I'm still not very good at it."[6]

Roald was so unhappy that he once faked appendicitis so he could go home. The family doctor in Llandaff knew Roald was pretending. However, the doctor was sensitive to the boy's homesickness. He let Roald stay at home for three days if he promised not to do it again.

Life at St. Peter's was not all bad. Roald was tall and strong, and his excellence at sports made him popular.

Roald, seen here in a class photo (third row up, fifth from right), was miserable at St. Peter's.

Also, Roald's love of reading helped him pass the time. He was especially fond of adventure writers such as Rudyard Kipling.

Furthermore, Roald could go home for holidays and the long summer vacation. These were wonderful times. The Dahls spent their summers in Norway, sailing in small boats, swimming, and picnicking.

## Roald and the Chocolate Factory

When Roald was thirteen he was sent to Repton, a famous boys' school in a part of England called Derbyshire. Roald hated Repton even more than St. Peter's. According to him, Repton's teachers were cruel, and Roald suffered through his classes in fear or boredom.

However, not everything was bad. One benefit was that the school was close to the Cadbury chocolate factory. Cadbury was, and still is, England's biggest chocolate

Two women put the finishing touches on chocolate Easter eggs at the Cadbury chocolate factory in 1932.

company. Occasionally the Repton boys became "tasters" for Cadbury. Each student was given a box with twelve new kinds of chocolate and asked to give his opinions.

This was heaven to Roald. He seriously considered becoming a chocolate-bar inventor, and he was obsessed with chocolate for the rest of his life. The experience also directly inspired one of his most famous books. When he was looking for a subject, he recalled, "I remembered those little cardboard boxes and the newly invented chocolates inside them, and I began to write a book called *Charlie and the Chocolate Factory.*"[7]

## "I Couldn't Wait"

Roald's mother offered to send him to university after he graduated from Repton. He was not interested, though. At age twenty, Roald was an eager young man, and he wanted to see the world. He took a job with Shell Oil because it promised him travel.

Roald spent two years in London, training for the job, before he got his wish: an assignment to East Africa. He later wrote, "I was off to the land of palm trees and coconuts and coral reefs and lions and elephants and deadly snakes, and a white hunter who had lived ten years in Mwanza [a city in East Africa] had told me that if a black mamba [snake] bit you, you died within the hour writhing in agony and foaming at the mouth. I couldn't wait."[8]

In those days just traveling to East Africa from England was an adventurous two-week boat trip. Roald left in the fall of 1938 aboard an old and noisy cargo ship. His adult life was beginning.

# Chapter Two

# Grand Adventures and Early Stories

Dahl stopped in many ports before reaching Dar es Salaam, the main city in Tanganyika (now Tanzania). He saw many colorful sights on this voyage. He described these in his book *Going Solo:* "What a lucky young fellow I was to be seeing all these marvelous places free of charge and with a good job at the end of it all."[9]

Dar es Salaam became Dahl's headquarters. He shared a house there with two other Shell employees. They supplied oil and gasoline to customers across East Africa.

Dahl traveled often on business, sometimes for a month at a time. On the African plains he saw wild animals and other amazing things. It was a good job for a curious person who liked the outdoors. He wrote, "Not a great deal of intelligence or imagination was required, but by gum you had to be fit and tough."[10]

Dahl also had several adventures at home. He watched a snake catcher capture a poisonous snake.

He also saw a lion carry off a woman in its jaws. Luckily a man with a rifle scared the animal away before it hurt her.

## Flying

After Dahl had been in Dar es Salaam about a year, war broke out. This was World War II, when England, France, and other countries fought against a group of nations led by Germany. Dahl became a British soldier in 1939.

He wanted to fly planes for the Royal Air Force (RAF). He was six feet six inches tall, and had trouble

As a young man, Dahl took a job with Shell Oil in Dar es Salaam, Tanganyika, in East Africa.

fitting into the cockpit of a fighter plane. The RAF needed pilots and agreed to take him anyway.

Being a fighter pilot was, and still is, a dangerous job. Out of the sixteen men in Dahl's flight class, thirteen died in the war. But flying was exciting and Dahl loved the adventure. Unfortunately, soon after graduating from flight school he had to make a crash landing in the North African desert.

Dahl was badly hurt. His nose was smashed into his skull. His legs and back were seriously injured. He needed several operations and months of recovery. The accident marked the end of Dahl's flying days. But it later inspired his first writing.

When World War II broke out in 1939, Dahl became a fighter pilot in the Royal Air Force.

# In America

Still an officer, Dahl was given a new job in the summer of 1941. England desperately needed help to defeat the Germans.

Dahl was sent to the British embassy in Washington, D.C. His job was to talk to important people about the war and try to get America to join with England in the fight. Dahl was good at this. He quickly became popular among the city's rich and powerful people.

The handsome, charming war hero was invited to many parties and receptions. He was known as an excellent guest who could talk intelligently about all sorts of things, from car mechanics to world politics. Dahl loved this life, and he loved the attention he received.

# "Shot Down over Libya"

One of Dahl's first tasks was to prepare an account of his crash in the Libyan desert. This story, "Shot Down over Libya," appeared in a popular magazine, the *Saturday Evening Post*, in August 1942. It was Dahl's first major published work.

The story was not a complete, true account of Dahl's crash, though. For example, its narrator is shot down by Italian fighter pilots. In reality, Dahl had to make a crash landing because he was given wrong directions and ran out of gas. He later said that an editor invented these false details. However, Dahl loved to **exaggerate**. He may have changed the facts himself to make the story more exciting.

In 1942 Dahl published this account of his crash landing in Libya in the *Saturday Evening Post.*

Dahl's next writing project was about **gremlins**. These were imaginary creatures that supposedly sabotaged RAF planes. RAF pilots had long blamed flying accidents and problems on mischievous gremlins.

Famous animated-movie producer Walt Disney wanted to make cartoons to help the war effort. He considered making one about Dahl's gremlins. This never happened, but in 1943 Disney published a picture book about them. The text was written by Flight Lieutenant Roald Dahl. This book, Dahl's first, is extremely rare today. A copy in good condition sells for thousands of dollars.

## Back to England

When World War II ended in 1945, Dahl returned to England. He settled in a village called Amersham. This put him close to his mother and sisters, who now had families of their own.

Dahl's experiences talking to people at Washington parties, and then writing about his crash and about gremlins, had taught him something. He realized he had a knack for telling vivid stories. He began using this talent to write short fiction. At that time popular magazines frequently published short stories. Dahl was often successful selling his work to these magazines.

Dahl's early stories were based on his experiences in Africa and in the

Dahl returned to England in 1945 and began writing stories about his experiences in the war.

war. All his life Dahl continued to collect incidents that could be made into fiction. He wrote these down in a small book he kept with him. Dahl's daughter Ophelia later commented, "He loved to collect things. When he was young it was birds' eggs and chocolate wrappers. As an adult he collected wine and paintings. However, he also collected ideas."[11]

In 1946 Dahl's first collection of stories, *Over to You,* was published. He then wrote *Sometime Never,* a novel about nuclear war—a new threat that had emerged at the end of World War II. The story collection did reasonably well, but the novel was not a success. Dahl decided to concentrate on short stories.

Dahl liked living in the English countryside and being near his adoring, attentive mother and sisters. However, he missed the sophisticated life he had led in America. He also knew he could sell stories more easily if he lived in New York City, the center of American publishing. So, at the beginning of the 1950s, Dahl moved there.

# Chapter Three

# Home and Family

B ack in America Dahl was delighted to once again be in a world of celebrities, artists, and rich people. He met and dated many attractive women. At a party in 1951, he met an actress, Patricia Neal.

Although she was ten years younger than Dahl, Neal was already a rising star on Broadway and in Hollywood. Her most famous role would come in the 1963 movie *Hud,* for which she won an Oscar. Dahl and Neal began dating regularly. They were married in 1953.

## Gipsy House

Dahl and Neal spent part of each year in America, but they also wanted to live in England. They hoped to raise a family in the countryside. The couple bought a home called Gipsy House in the village of Great Missenden near London.

Dahl loved this house, which was surrounded by gardens and orchards. It was beautiful, close to the rest of Dahl's family, and far from the intensity of New York. He wrote to a friend, "It's marvelous, isolated, quiet."[12]

In 1953 Dahl married the American actress Patricia Neal.

Dahl put all his energy into making Gipsy House perfect. He collected and cared for a variety of farm animals. He kept a garden with about one hundred kinds of roses. He built a huge enclosure in which dozens of small birds could fly freely.

He also fixed up an old **gypsy caravan**, a small wooden house on wheels. This later became a playhouse for the couple's children: Olivia (1955), Tessa (1957), Theo (1960), Ophelia (1964), and Lucy (1965).

## The Writing Hut

Dahl also remodeled a gardening shed. He wanted to use this as a writing hut. The cozy space was perfect for Dahl, except he needed to keep the hut's windows closed. Otherwise, cows put their heads in and chewed the curtains.

Dahl spent hours in his hut every day. He typically wrote all morning. After lunch he fed the animals, played with his children, and took walks. He usually wrote again before dinner.

When working, Dahl sat in an old armchair. He was surrounded by a collection of strange and wonderful objects. These included pieces of bone from his own back, reminders of his many operations. Dahl usually wrapped his legs in a blanket for warmth and propped his feet on a heavy trunk. Then he put a writing board covered in green cloth on his lap and wrote in pencil.

Dahl wrote all of his children's stories in this hut in the garden of his home near London.

Writing was slow work for Dahl. He finished only about two stories a year. He took a long time thinking up the ideas for his stories, and he spent a long time revising them. Each one had to be perfect.

Dahl's short stories continued to be fairly popular. But Neal's acting jobs always made more money for the family. Major success did not come for Dahl until he turned his attention to a new audience: children.

## James and Charlie

The first of his books for kids, *James and the Giant Peach,* was inspired by the blackbirds that ate the cherries in Dahl's orchard. He imagined a fruit that was so big that no bird could eat it.

It took a long time for Dahl to develop this idea into a story. He said, "It was a tiny seed of an idea. I walked around it, looked at it, and sniffed it for a long time."[13] Eventually, though, he turned this little idea into a story

A giant mechanical shark attacks James and his peach in the 1996 Disney version of *James and the Giant Peach.*

The cast of the 1971 film *Willy Wonka and the Chocolate Factory* poses for a group photo.

about a boy who discovers a magical peach. The peach grows so large that the boy can get inside it. It takes him, and an odd group of talking insects, across the ocean.

Dahl told this tale to his children as a bedtime story, but he did not think it was good enough to become a book. However, his kids loved it so much that Dahl agreed to send it to his publisher. The publisher also loved it and agreed to print it.

Even before *James* was published, Dahl began a second book for kids. This was *Charlie and the Chocolate Factory*. The story was about a poor boy who wins a fabulous prize. He gets a tour of a magical chocolate factory with his grandfather and some selfish, greedy children.

This book was inspired by the writer's schoolboy experience with testing chocolate and by his lifelong love of the candy. Dahl loved chocolate so much that he joked it should be a subject for study: "If I were a headmaster, I would get rid of the history teacher and get a chocolate teacher instead."[14]

## Tragedies

Dahl's first children's books began to sell well. Writing them was fun, and Dahl enjoyed it a lot. In the early 1960s, though, his new career was put off course by three tragedies.

First, in 1960 a taxi hit Theo's stroller in a busy New York street. The baby lived, but he suffered serious brain damage. The family retreated to England, which seemed safer than New York. There, in 1961, Olivia, age seven, died of **German measles**. At the time, few English children were **inoculated** against this disease.

The family was heartbroken. Even Dahl, who was normally strong, cheerful, and energetic, became deeply depressed. Six months after Olivia's death, he wrote to his publishers, "I feel right now as though I'll never in my life do any more! I simply cannot seem to get started again."[15]

Then, in 1965 Dahl's wife suffered a stroke. This happens when a blood vessel near the brain bursts. Neal survived, but afterward could not speak well, remember things clearly, or walk without help. She was pregnant at the time, but the baby, Lucy, was born normal.

Dahl never liked to sit still, and one way he handled difficulty in his life was to bury himself in helping others. For instance, Dahl tackled one of Theo's medical problems. Fluid that built up near the baby's brain had to be drained regularly. Unfortunately, the

Neal, seen here after her stroke in 1965, is surrounded by her family: (left to right) Theo, Dahl, Ophelia, and Tessa.

**valve** doctors inserted inside Theo's head kept clogging. Every time this happened, an operation was needed.

Dahl asked for help from two friends, a surgeon and an engineer who designed tiny mechanisms. Together they created an improved valve. This device helped thousands of children.

Dahl also helped his wife to overcome her stroke. He organized friends and neighbors so someone was with her all day, every day, coaching her in speech and movement. Eventually Neal recovered well enough to act again.

# Chapter Four

# Roald Dahl's Legacy

No matter what he was doing—working, playing, or helping others—Dahl devoted himself completely to it. Much of this restless energy now went toward making money. His children were growing up, and for years he was the only one in the family who could work. Dahl wanted to make sure his family never had to worry about finances.

To reach this goal he wrote two **screenplays**. One was for the James Bond movie *You Only Live Twice*, and the other was for the children's movie *Chitty Chitty Bang Bang*. Both were hits, and Dahl's earnings were large. Neal would tell friends, "Do you know he made more writing that one [Bond] movie than I ever made in my career?" Then she would tease her husband by adding, "Although *I* won the Oscar."[16]

Even more financially successful was the movie version of Dahl's book about Charlie. The film was retitled *Willy Wonka and the Chocolate Factory*, and it made Dahl a small fortune. Still, Dahl hated it.

Among other things, he disliked the choice of actor to play Willy Wonka.

## "Reaching into His Imagination"

The success of the *Willy Wonka* movie made Dahl a household name around the world. He grew increasingly wealthy, popular, and famous. As always, Dahl loved the attention. He liked to boast that he would be recognized if he walked into any house in England or America, as long as it had children.

From the late 1960s into the 1980s, Dahl continued to write books for kids. Titles from this period include *Fantastic Mr. Fox, Charlie and the Great Glass*

Dahl was unhappy with the choice to cast Gene Wilder (seated) as Willy Wonka in the film.

*Elevator, Matilda, The Twits, Danny the Champion of the World, The Witches,* and *Revolting Rhymes.* Almost every one of them was a hit.

One reason kids love these books is because of a partnership Dahl formed in the late 1970s with a new illustrator, Quentin Blake. Before they teamed up, many other artists had made drawings for Dahl's books. But the combination of Dahl and Blake was magical. Their styles perfectly matched. After their first book together (*The Enormous Crocodile*) Blake's illustrations added their own liveliness to nearly all of Dahl's books.

One of Dahl's best-known books is *The BFG.* It is about a Big Friendly Giant (BFG) with a goofy way of talking who captures dreams in jars and blows them

James talks with the grasshopper, spider, and ladybug in a scene from *James and the Giant Peach.*

into children's bedrooms. The BFG teams up with a girl named Sophie to defeat evil giants and visit the queen of England. As he often did, Dahl wove his own life into this story. Sophie was named after his first grandchild. Also, the BFG's wacky speech was inspired by the language Dahl's wife used just after her stroke, before she relearned how to speak properly.

All of Dahl's many books began as bedtime stories told to his youngest children (Ophelia and Lucy) or to his granddaughter Sophie. Ophelia recalls, "Every evening after my sister Lucy and I had gone to bed, my father would walk slowly up the stairs, his bones creaking louder than the staircase, to tell us a story. I can see him now, leaning against the wall of our bedroom with his hands in his pockets looking into the distance, reaching into his imagination."[17]

## Troubles

Despite fame and success during the later decades of his life, Dahl had many troubles. For one thing, his physical problems worsened. He had to have two more operations on his back, one on his nose, and another to replace a hip. He moved slowly and was in constant pain.

Sometimes Dahl created his own troubles. Dahl loved to shock people, saying wild things to make them think. He once wrote a book review that was critical of Israel. Some people considered his statements harsh and **anti-Semitic**. Many people then refused to buy his books. And some booksellers refused to carry them in their stores.

Although Dahl developed serious health problems later in life, he continued to write books.

In 1967 Dahl's spirit was crushed when his mother died. He had been close to her all his life. He remarked later, "She was undoubtedly the absolute primary influence on my own life. She had a crystal-clear intellect and a deep interest in almost everything under the sun."[18]

Perhaps the greatest distress in Dahl's life during this period, though, was the breakup of his marriage. It had always been stormy, and after thirty years it finally ended. Dahl had fallen in love with another woman: Felicity Ann Crosland, nicknamed Liccy (pronounced "Lissy"). She and Dahl married in 1983.

## Active Until the End

Despite his various problems, Dahl remained active. Even after he was diagnosed with a form of **leukemia** (a serious blood disease), Dahl did not like to stay still. Nor did he have patience with others who were idle. Lucy Dahl recalls her father "didn't want anything to do with anyone who sat around and moaned."[19]

Dahl spent his time as he chose. As he had all his life, he enjoyed fine food and wine. He refused to give up smoking, despite his doctor's advice. He still worked in his vegetable garden and picked mushrooms in the woods.

This 1987 photograph shows Dahl, his second wife Felicity (center), his daughter Tessa, and his grandson Luke.

Dahl also organized friends to play a weekly game of **snooker,** which is similar to pool. He spent hours every day writing replies to the fan letters he received from children around the world. And he continued to write books. One of the last he wrote was *The Vicar of Nibbleswicke,* a fiendishly funny book about a clergyman who pronounces all the most important words backwards (for example, he offers praise to Dog).

Roald Dahl died of leukemia on November 23, 1990, in a hospital in Oxford, England. He was seventy-four. Dahl was buried on a hillside near his beloved Gipsy House.

## Roald Dahl's Legacy

In several ways, however, Dahl continues to live. His books grow more popular all the time. Over 1 million are sold every year. In 1999 a survey of fifteen thousand children ages seven to eleven placed four of Dahl's books among the top ten kids' books ever written. *Matilda* was voted number one, and the list also included *Charlie and the Chocolate Factory, The Twits,* and *The BFG.*

Meanwhile, several new film and stage versions of his books have been made. An excellent movie of *The Witches* was made in 1990. Equally successful films of *James and the Giant Peach* and *Matilda* came out in 1996. A remake of *Charlie and the Chocolate Factory* is scheduled for 2005, with actor Johnny Depp starring as Willy Wonka.

Dahl's name is being kept alive in other ways as well. Roald Dahl Children's Gallery is a permanent exhibit in a

Matilda argues with her mother in a scene from the 1996 film
version of *Matilda*.

museum near Dahl's home in Great Missenden, England.
Through hands-on displays, Dahl's best-known characters help children discover the wonders of science.

Also, after her husband's death Felicity Dahl estab-
lished the Roald Dahl Foundation. This organization
gives money to groups involved in subjects that interested
him, such as **literacy,** music, and medical research. And so
Dahl's name remains familiar. New generations of children will delight in his books for years to come.

# Notes

Introduction: The Champion Storyteller

1. Quoted in Jubilee Books, "Jubilee Books—Roald Dahl Profile," www.jubileebooks.co.uk.
2. Quoted in William H. Honan, "Roald Dahl, Writer, 74, Is Dead; Best Sellers Enchanted Children," *New York Times*, November 24, 1990. Reprinted on RoaldDahlFans.com, www.roalddahl fans.com.
3. Quoted in Honan, "Roald Dahl, Writer, 74, Is Dead."
4. Quoted in Jubilee Books, "Jubilee Books—Roald Dahl Profile."

Chapter One: A Boy in Wales

5. Roald Dahl, *Boy.* New York: Farrar, Straus & Giroux, 1984, p. 22.
6. Roald Dahl, *My Year.* New York: Viking, 1994, p. 56.
7. Dahl, *Boy,* p. 135.
8. Dahl, *Boy,* p. 159.

Chapter Two: Grand Adventures and Early Stories

9. Roald Dahl, *Going Solo.* New York: Farrar, Straus & Giroux, 1984, p. 31.
10. Dahl, *Going Solo,* p. 35.
11. Quoted in Jubilee Books, "Memories of the Man," www.jubileebooks.co.uk.

## Chapter Three: Home and Family

12. Quoted in Jeremy Treglown, *Roald Dahl: A Biography*. New York: Farrar, Straus & Giroux, 1994, p. 126.
13. Quoted in Lucy Dahl, *James and the Giant Peach: The Book and Movie Scrapbook*. New York: Disney Press, 1996, p. 4.
14. Felicity Dahl and Roald Dahl, *Memories with Food at Gipsy House*. New York: Viking, 1991, p. 154.
15. Quoted in Treglown, *Roald Dahl: A Biography*, p. 148.

## Chapter Four: Roald Dahl's Legacy

16. Patricia Neal, *As I Am: An Autobiography*. New York: Simon & Schuster, 1988, p. 291.
17. Quoted in Jubilee Books, "Jubilee Books—Roald Dahl Profile."
18. Dahl and Dahl, *Memories*, p. 65.
19. Quoted in Treglown, *Roald Dahl: A Biography*, p. 276.

# Glossary

**anti-Semitic:** Prejudiced against Jewish people.

**appendicitis:** An inflammation of the appendix, which is part of the digestive tract. Today, this disease is treatable.

**exaggerate:** To make something seem more than it really is.

**German measles:** A sometimes deadly disease. Most children in the world today get a vaccination to prevent it.

**gremlins:** Mischievous, imaginary creatures that supposedly sabotaged the airplanes of the Royal Air Force in World War II.

**gypsy caravan:** A little wooden house on wheels, once used by traveling bands of gypsies.

**headmasters:** The principals of British schools.

**inoculated:** Medically protected by an injection against certain diseases.

**leukemia:** A serious and often deadly blood disease.

**literacy:** The ability to read and write.

**pneumonia:** A lung disease. Today it can usually be easily treated.

**screenplays:** The scripts used to make movies.

**snooker:** A game, popular in England, similar to pool.

**valve:** A device that allows liquid to flow one way or to be shut off.

# For Further Exploration

## Books

Lucy Dahl, *James and the Giant Peach: The Book and Movie Scrapbook*. New York: Disney Press, 1996. Written by one of Dahl's daughters, this book details the writing of one of Dahl's best-loved books and, later, the making of the movie version.

Roald Dahl, *Boy*. New York: Farrar, Straus & Giroux, 1984. This memoir about the author's boyhood is written to appeal to both adults and young readers.

———, *Going Solo*. New York: Farrar, Straus & Giroux, 1984. Continuing his memoirs, Dahl takes readers through his adventures in World War II.

———, *My Year*. New York: Viking, 1994. This collection of short essays about each month of the year includes many memories of Dahl's youth.

Chris Powling, *Tell Me About: Roald Dahl*. Minneapolis: Carolrhoda Books, 1997. A very simple biography written for young readers.

## Web Sites

**Bucks CC—County Museum—Roald Dahl Children's Gallery** (www.buckscc.gov.uk). This site has photos and short descriptions of the things visitors can see at the permanent museum exhibit honoring Dahl.

**Jubilee Books** (www.jubileebooks.co.uk). This Web site, maintained by a British book company, has

information on Dahl and many good quotes from
him, his friends, and his family.

**Official Roald Dahl Web Site** (www.roalddahl.com).
This terrific interactive site has biographical information about Dahl as well as lots of fun stuff.

**RoaldDahlFans.com** (www.roalddahlfans.com). This
site is maintained by a fan of Dahl's books. It has
games and other fun activities in addition to information about the man and his work.

# Index

# Picture Credits

# About the Author

Adam Woog has written more than forty books for adults, young adults, and children. Among his works for KidHaven Press are books about Steven Spielberg, Bill Gates, cowboys, and medieval knights. He lives in Seattle, Washington, with his wife and their daughter.